It's Your Business!

How to build and grow an award winning real estate business.

A PUBLICATION OF MOREGCI
BY: JOHN MOSCILLO

www.MoreGCI.com

Blank for Note Taking

TABLE OF CONTENTS

Overview

MORE GCI

Every business must ask itself:
Four important Questions

---

1. **What is our vision?**

2. **What is our purpose?**

3. **What are our goals?**

4. **What is our exit strategy?**

Did you know:

•4 out of 5 small businesses fail. The majority of the remaining businesses are dying a slow death.

•80% of agents fail in the first year. What about the other 20%? In their second year, 80% of them fail to achieve a sustainable business, as well.

•The majority of small business owners create a job for themselves with no residual income or exit strategy. Simply put, if they stop working, the income stops coming in.

•In order to achieve success in business, you must understand your business. You must work ON your business, not just IN it.

It is not about doing the work that is required, we all need to do that work. It is about spending time on your creation. Through working on your creation you will find passion through the vision which will lead to purpose. No one can decide when and where that purpose comes from or when it will come but it will only come from working on your business as a business owner.

Once you have a vision and passion, it is only then that you will achieve the success you desire through the purpose.

There is only one obstacle standing between you and success…

That obstacle is **YOU**.
> Your Fear
> Your Lack of Confidence
> Your Lack of Business Knowledge
> Your Lack of Planning
> Your Lack of Understanding
> Your Lack of Action
> Your Lack of Discipline

Once you remove YOU as the obstacle, anything is possible.

The Power of YOU

Most people look at the word YOU as the individual self. When you look at YOU as something greater than the individual then explosive growth happens.

Y – Your Big "Y"
O – Organization of goals and action plans
U – Utilization of systems and people around your to accomplish goals.

Business

The Three Levels of Business

In order for a business to be successful it is important to understand the aspects of a business and the responsibilities of each level.

In Michael Gerber's 'The E-Myth' he states businesses are defined by 3 distinct levels:

1.   **The Entrepreneur**
2.   **The Manager**
3.   **The Technician**

You are not just an agent, you are a business owner. It is crucial for your success to Understand, Separate and Perform at all 3 levels. Failure to do so will create a weak link in your organization and, ultimately, it will end in Frustration, a Plateau and possibly Failure.

In a percentage amount, how much time do you spend in the following
(must equal 100%)

Entrepreneur Level   _____%

Manager Level   _____%

Technical Level   _____%

Vision vs. Purpose

What is your Vision?

What is your Purpose?

From Vision, the Purpose will arise but Purpose can never supply the Vision.*

Take some time to think about what your Vision is; write it down and read it often.

In one or two sentences, answer the following:

What is your vision?_____

_____

_____

What is your purpose?_____

_____

_____

---

* Michael Gerber E-Myth Mastery

Entrepreneur
Provides the idea and overall
vision of the business

Management
Understands, Plans and Brings
the vision to fruition

Technician
Carries out the duties to
accomplish the vision

Vision
(Where the Passion Lives)

CEO & President

Who is your CEO?

_____

Purpose
(Understands, Plans and Brings
the vision to fruition)

*VP's, Finance Manager, Sales
Manager*

Who is your Manager?

_____

Job
(This is where most agents focus)

*Sales People, Web Dev Team,
Customer Service,
Administration, etc.*

Who are your Technicians?

_____

Introduction to
The UPAD Principles of Success

U	**P**
Understanding	Planning
Action	Discipline
A	**D**

Understanding

The first point you must focus on in these principles is **Understanding**.

It is only then that you can start to generate a plan for success. You must Know and Understand:

• What GCI is needed to attain your goals.
• *Number of Sides needed to attain your goals.*
• What your Average Sales Price is at any given time.
• Your Conversion Ratio and where to best spend time and money as well as where your business comes from.
• Your Average Commission and if there's any way to capitalize and maximize each sale.
• How much you need to sell in order to pay yourself what you want, after expenses.

By understanding exactly what is required to achieve your goals, you will able to implement the next principle, **Planning**.

Planning

Now that you **Understand** what is required, you can make a **Plan** on how to get there.

•How you will get your required number of sides?
•How you will get the required number of appointments?
•How you will achieve your production numbers?
•How you will make the required number of calls or contacts?
•Who are your referral partners and what expectations do you have?
•How many luncheons you will go on with referral partners?

So with a full **Understanding** of what is required and a **Plan** in place, you are now able to move to the next principle, **Action**.

Action

By carrying out the **Plan**…. The **Action** is simply doing the work you planned because you **Understand** what is required.

- Booking appointments
- Making calls
- Door Knocking
- Following Up
- Writing deals
- Closing deals
- Getting referrals
- Asking everyone for business
  - Wait staff, Postal Workers, Landscapers, Movers, Contractors, Bankers, Pizza Delivery, Business Owners, Friends, Family, Insurance Agents, Financial Planners, Attorneys… The list goes on and on

Now that you **Understand**, have a **Plan** and are in **Action**, you are ready for the next principle, **Discipline.**

Discipline

The hardest principal of all is the ability to shut off distractions and stay on track with what you have **Planned** and what is required to achieve your goal. Keep your **Action** flowing and do the things **you do not want to do, but must!**

- Get to work early
- Pick up the phone and connect with people, no excuses
- No extended lunches, except on occasion and only if you are on track; unless there is a referral in it or it is with a client
- Stay PRODUCTIVE not just Busy
- Stay proactive and ready at any time
- Go to BNI, Chambers, Rotary, Kiwanis, Charity events, even though you may be uncomfortable
- Identify high impact activities and only do these until you hit your goal and close any negative GAP's

The difference between *Successful* and *Highly Successful* people is the discipline to do what you DO NOT want to do so, eventually, you can **ONLY** do what you want to do!

UPAD and the 3 tiers

<u>Entrepreneur</u>

Your Entrepreneurial spark has brought you to this point.
You have the vision to be a top producing agent or build a team, and build a business in real estate. As the Entrepreneur, it is your overall view of the organization you are creating.

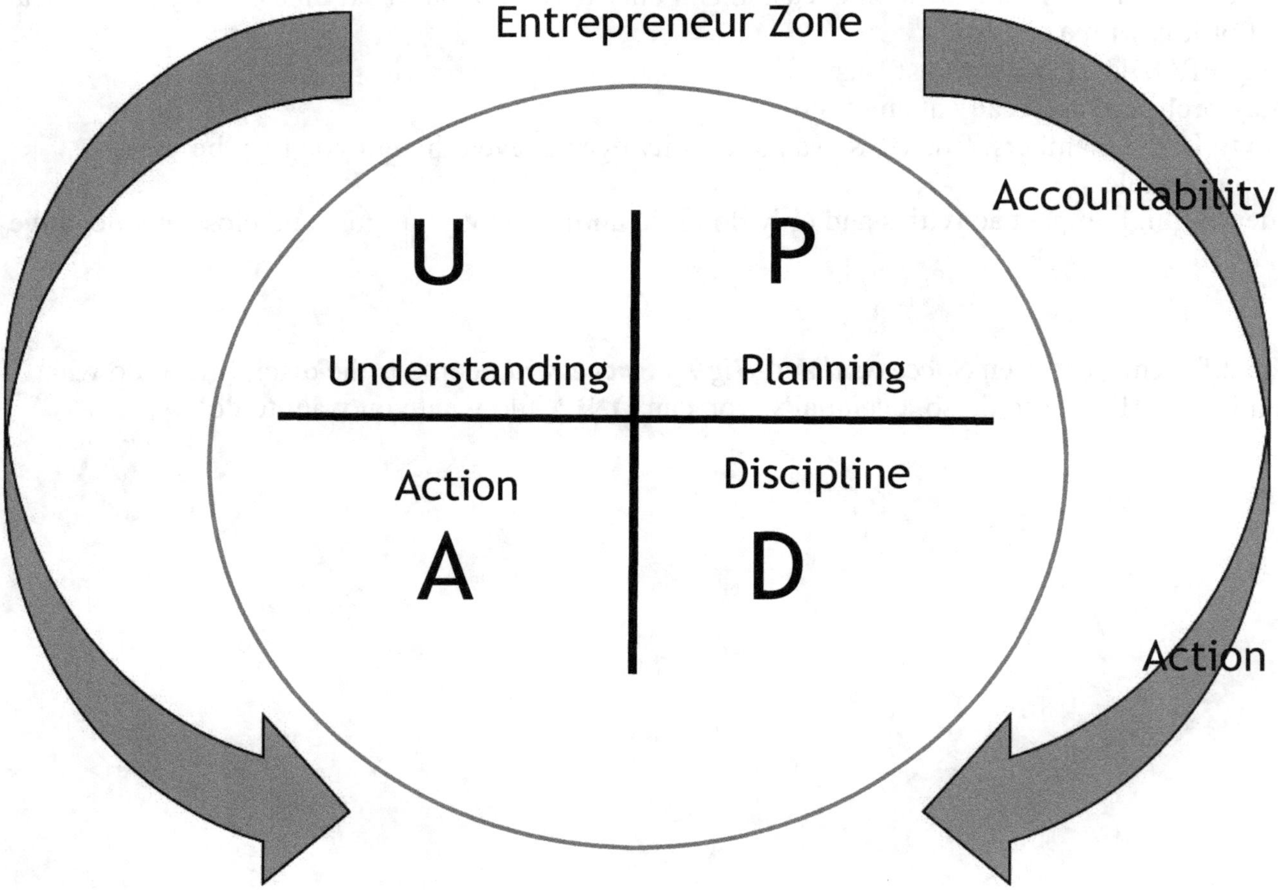

Entrepreneur Zone

Accountability

U — Understanding
P — Planning

Action — A
Discipline — D

Action

Manager

As the Manager, your job is to Understand the business's needs, Plan Goals, create Action Plans to achieve those goals and to organize and hold accountable your Sales Force, the Technicians.

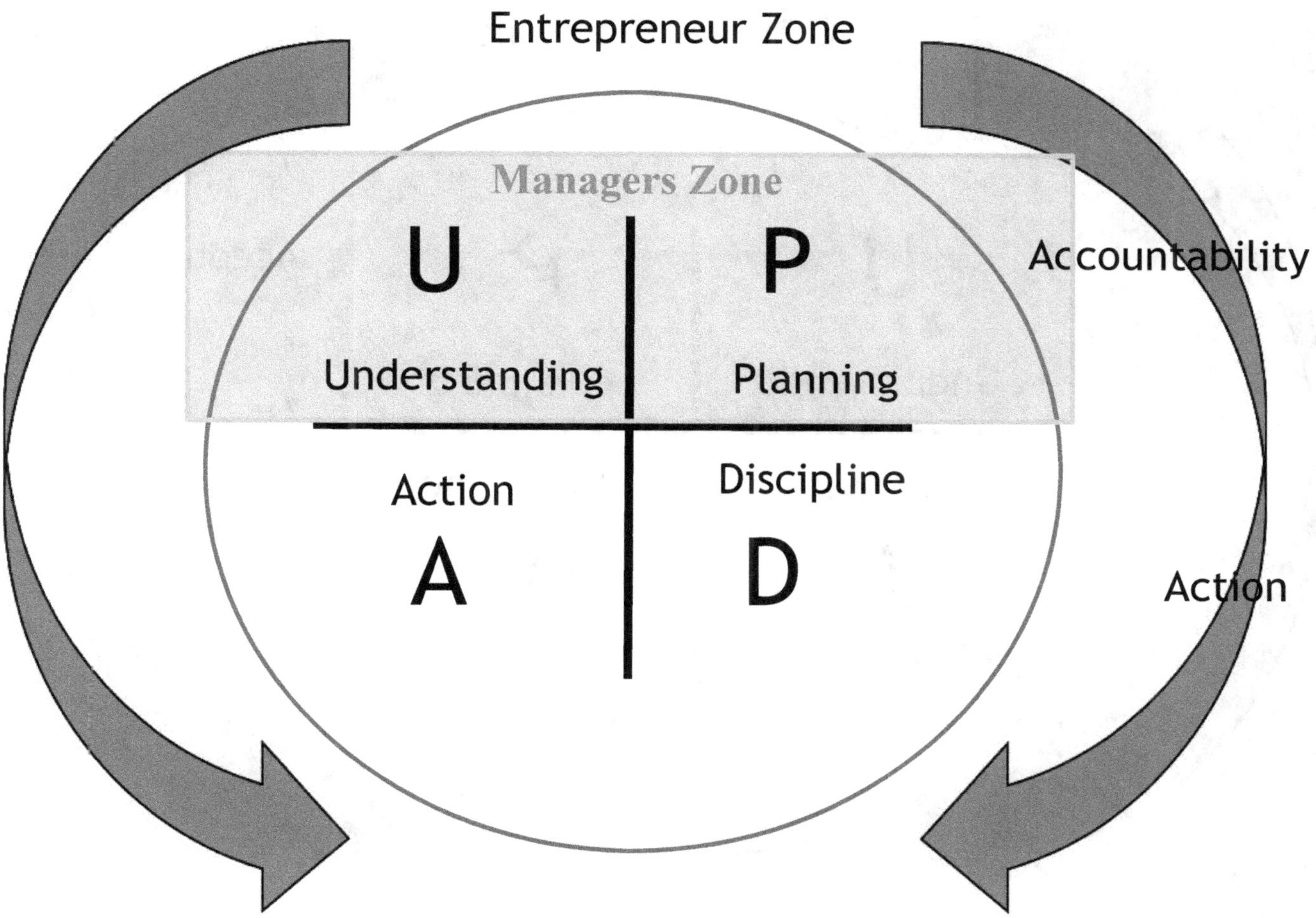

Entreprenur Zone

Managers Zone

U — Understanding

P — Planning

A — Action

D — Discipline

Accountability

Action

Technician

In the role of the Technician, or Sales Person, it is your job to implement the goals of the organization and put them into Action. You must also have the Discipline to continue following the plan in order to accomplish the goals of the organization. This is where we spend the majority of our time and where there may be a disconnect.

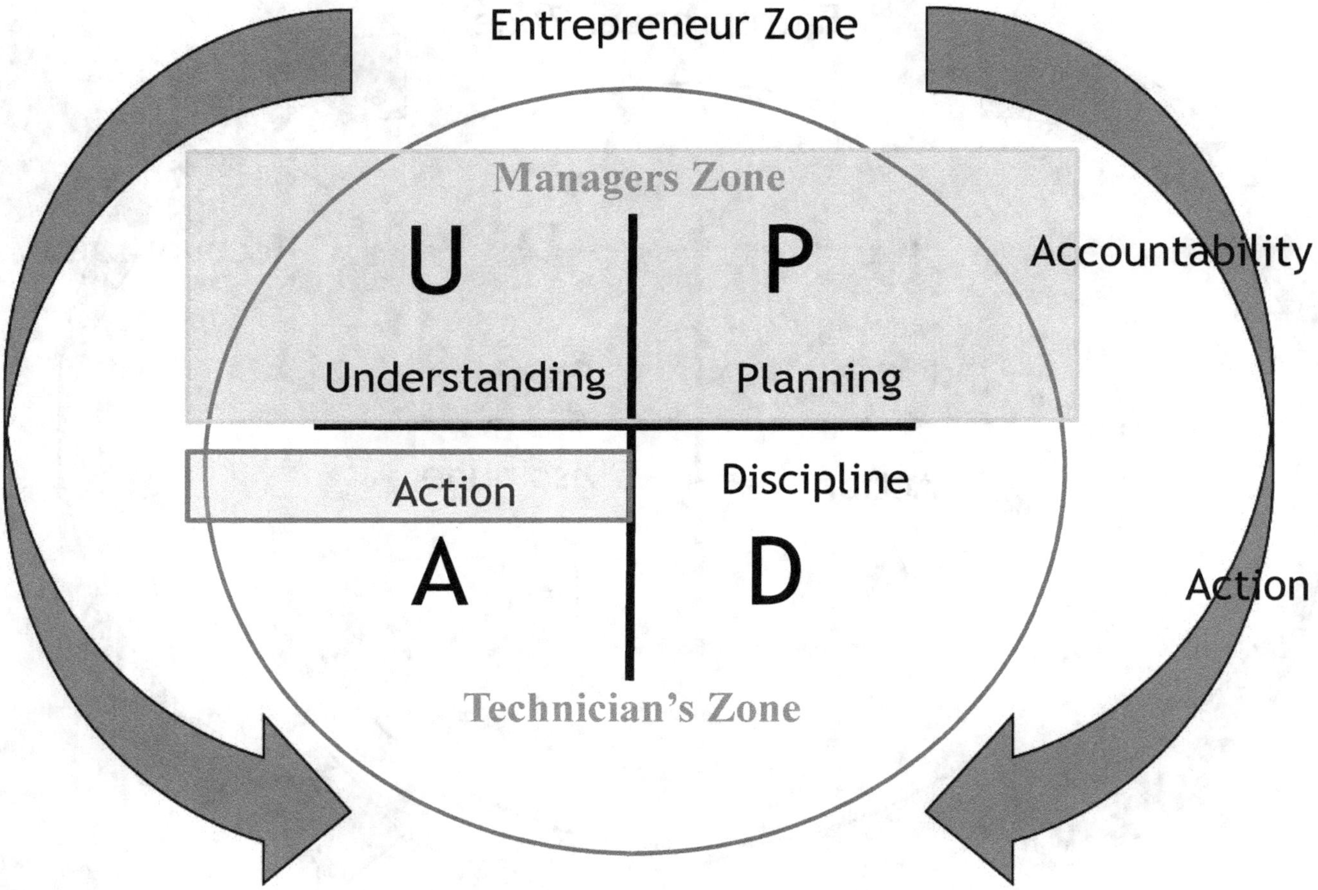

Entrepreneur Zone

Managers Zone

U
Understanding

P
Planning

Accountability

Action

Discipline

A

D

Action

Technician's Zone

The Disconnect

Discipline is connected to Accountability on the Management level. Most agents do not have accountability partners or do not have management level accountability. As a result they easily loose focus and can veer off track from their goals.

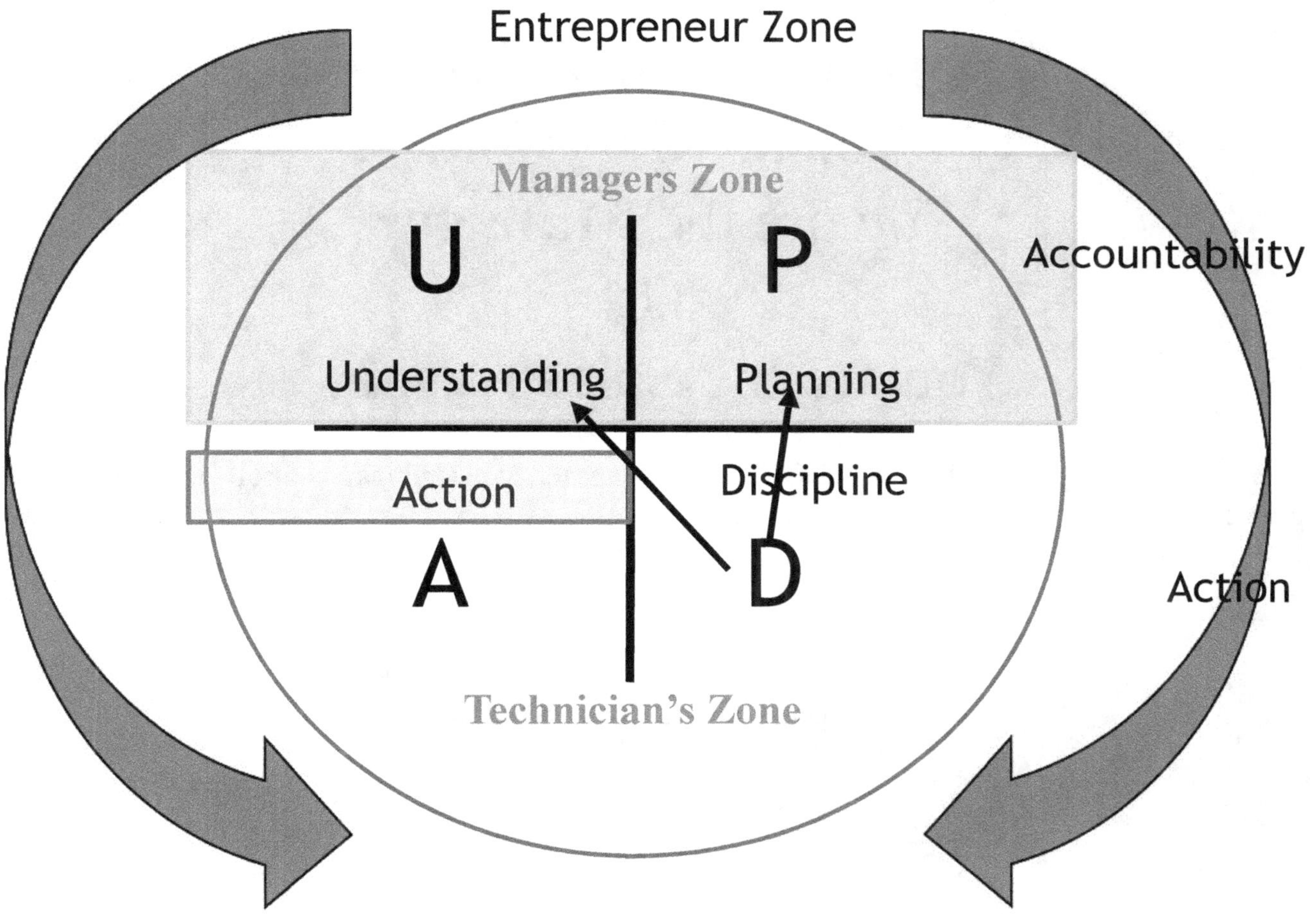

Entrepreneur Zone

Managers Zone

U   **P**

Understanding   Planning

Accountability

Action   Discipline

A   **D**

Action

Technician's Zone

When you **Understand** and **Plan** your business as a *Manager* and as a *Technician*, you will be able to put **Discipline** into **Action**. You will achieve success in your business and bring the *Entrepreneurial* vision to fruition.

Failure to **Understand** and **Plan** your business will leave you blind and frustrated. You may achieve a level of success without **Action** and **Discipline**, but you will not reach your full potential and will eventually come to a plateau or, even worse, a screeching halt all together. The *Manager and Technician's* responsibility is to implement the *Entrepreneur's Vision.*

You are the **CEO**,
You are the **CFO**,
You are the **Manager**
and
You are the **Salesperson.**

When you use the power of the More GCI Agent Manager, you will take control of your business and create a solid management level.

Be Accountable… Be Successful.

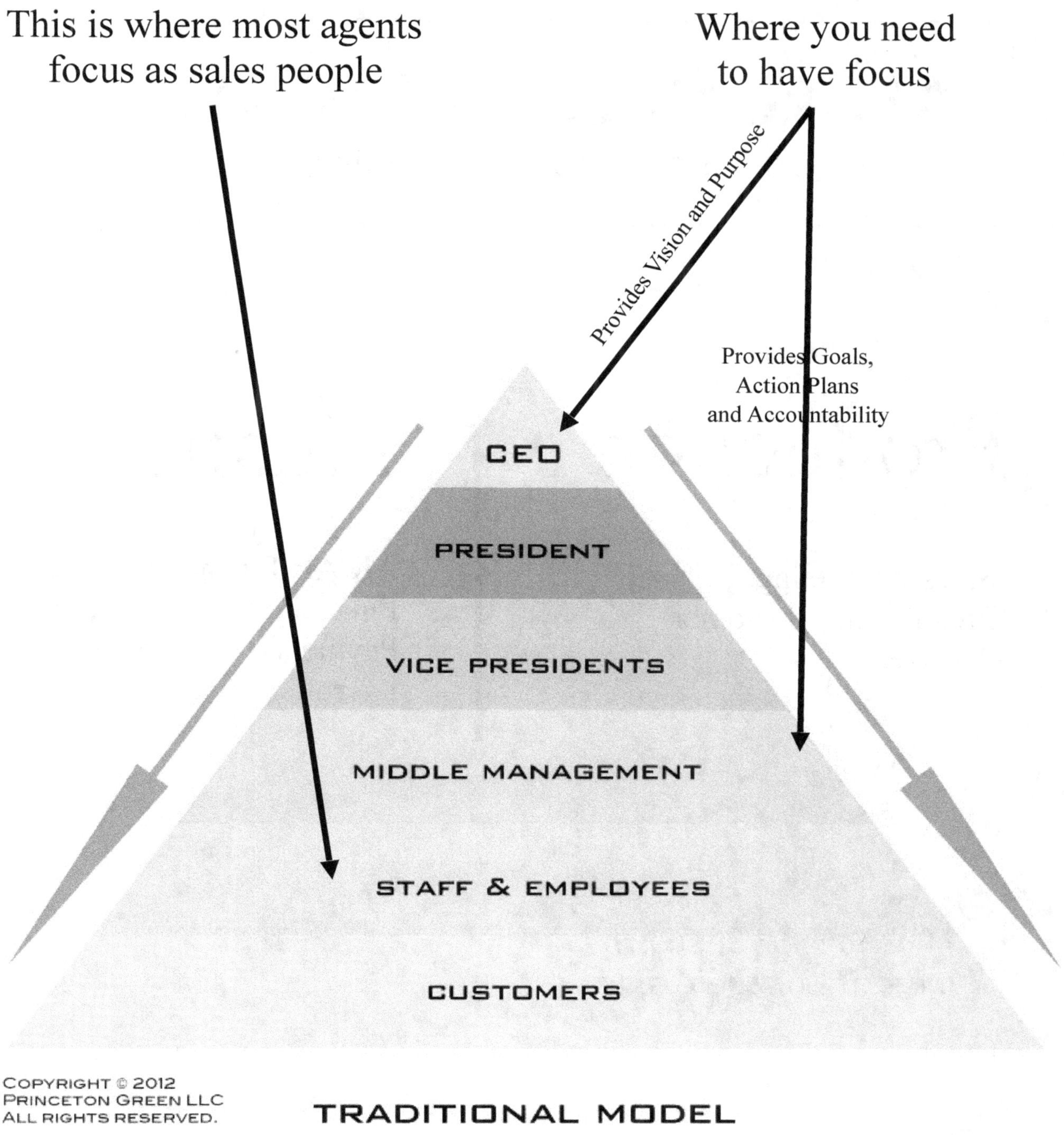

This is where most agents
focus as sales people

Where you need
to have focus

Provides Vision and Purpose

Provides Goals,
Action Plans
and Accountability

CEO

PRESIDENT

VICE PRESIDENTS

MIDDLE MANAGEMENT

STAFF & EMPLOYEES

CUSTOMERS

TRADITIONAL MODEL

MORE
GCI

ALL Real Estate Businesses
Have Two Distinct Sides

Production

Finance

Sales, Marketing,
Prospecting, Customer
Service,

AR/AP, Financial Goals,
Financial Well Being, Tax
Payments, Retirement,
Payroll

*(Most agents spend the
majority of their time
here)*

- If you want to increase your business by 20%, 30%, 50%, 100%, 300% - you must focus on the Financial Side of your business.

- This is the side of the business that determines the Financial Goals and well being of a company.

- They determine Sales Goals and give them to the Sales Department – Production Side – for fulfillment.

- The goals are then tracked for progress by Management.

How often do you look at the numbers of your business Be honest. How many times week or month do you review the numbers?

       Per Week _____

       Per Month _____

A Good Manager Will Tell You

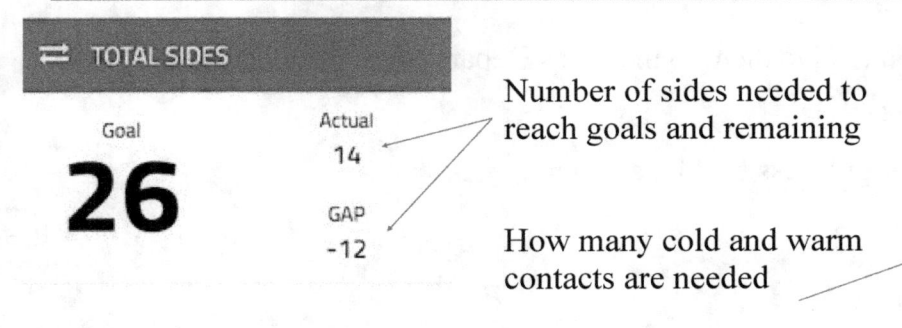

⇄ TOTAL SIDES

Goal
26

Actual
14

GAP
-12

To Goal: 53%

Number of sides needed to reach goals and remaining

☎ OUTBOUND CONTACTS

Warm Contacts
Year: 1,104
Month: 92
Week: 21

[−] 29 [+]

Cold Contacts
Year: 4,415
Month: 368
Week: 85

[−] 19 [+]

How many cold and warm contacts are needed

$ TOTAL PRODUCTION i +

Goal
$8,000,000

Actual
$4,228,000

GAP
-$3,772,000

To Goal: 53%

What your production goal is and how much more is needed

📅 APPOINTMENTS i +

Year Goal	Month Goal	Week Goal
55.2	4.6	1.1
Year Actual	Month Actual	Week Actual
23	0	0
Year Gap	Month Gap	Week Gap
-32.2	-4.6	-1.1

How many appointments you need and track them

✓ LEADS i +

Zbuyer	1	100%
SOI	1	100%
Referral - Past Client - ...	1	100%
Referral - ISA - Mike	1	100%
Referral - From Agent	2	100%

What your lead conversion ratio is

🏠 AVERAGE SALES PRICE

$302,000

What your average commission is and what you are leaving on the table

MORE GCI

A Good Manager will also...

...track the progress to your goals and let you know about any GAP.

GCI Goal: $200,000   YTD: $74,820   GAP: $125,180   % To Goal: 37.41%

...hold you accountable to lead generate and give you a progress report on future and potential earnings.

HIT LIST	
Thomas and Marilyn	6/15/17
Stephen	6/17/17
Chris and Beverly	6/23/17
Dena and Andy	7/5/17
James and Rose	7/7/17

UNDER CONTRACT	
Production	Sides
$1,263,900	4
Commission $	Commission %
$31,572.50	2.50%

PIPELINE
$2,567,900
CARMELENE
Ed
Colleen
Craig and Robyn

Current Leads   **Potential Business**   **Future Income**

MORE
GCI

SWOT Analysis

Take a moment and do a quick SWOT analysis. This takes a little critical thinking and honesty on your part. Think about each section and write down corresponding answers.

For example, if your **Strength** is being Personable and Well Liked, then write it down.

If your **Weakness** is Technology, Follow-Up or Networking Events, write it down.

What are your current and future **Opportunities**?

What are the **Threats**? A changing market? Another agent/firm? Your own mind?

Once you are able to see your honest SWOT, you can make the needed adjustments. Think like an Entrepreneur, Manager and Sales Person.

Strength	Weakness
Opportunity	Threat

Financial

Blank for Note Taking

Many agents have no idea what they need to make and when they receive a commission check, they treat it as pay day and fly by the seat of their pants. During the good months, they have a stock pile of cash and use it to pay taxes, past bills and take vacations. Then they struggle in the slow months and often may end up in tax trouble.

You now need to tap into the CFO of your business but before you do, you need to create a Personal Budget and a Business Budget. A simple budget which has all your bills accounted for. This gives you what your take home NEEDS to be.

Think about this for a moment. When a software salesperson sells a bundle of software, the company makes money. The salesperson gets a percentage of that, and not the whole thing. Treat your business in the same manner.

Needs and Wants - both Personal and Business

Needs - Personal
Mortgage / Rent
Utilities
Groceries

Wants - Personal
Estate planning
Retirement
Recreational vehicles

Needs – Business
Monthly fees
Advertising
Signs

Wants – Business
Customer appreciation events
Newest technology and equipment
Team / Support staff

Below is an example of a simple spreadsheet. In this scenario, you need to make $51,240 at a minimum, to break even for your personal and business sectors. Adjust to your requirements.

Budgets						
Personal				Business		
Rent	1500			KW Monthly	200	
Auto Gas	500			NNEREN	25	
Insurance	95			Dialer	125	
Cell	250			Call Capture	50	
Credit Cards	500			Signs Service	90	
Oil	100			Web Advertising	200	
Braces	235					
Taxes	200					
Student Loan	200					
	3,580				690	

Save for later

Pay Day

Utilizing the spreadsheet formula, you now have the amounts associated to each account. You can change this to any formula that suits your life and business. Notice that not all the commission goes to your personal account.

	Break Down		
	Check Amount	5,000	
	Percent of each sale	Avg amt per sale	
Taxes	20.00%	1,000	
Business	10.00%	500	
Retirement	5.00%	250	
Insurances	2.00%	100	
Rainy Day	2.00%	100	
Savings	6.00%	300	
Leisure	3.00%	150	
Personal Income	52.00%	2,600	
	100.0%		

Once you complete your budget, you can create and implement an action plan.

Commission Check

Required amounts are transferred to associated accounts

Accounts
•Taxes
•Retirement
•Rainy Day
•Savings
•Vacation
•Insurances

**Business Account
(Pay business bills)**

True personal income – Net Income

Personal Account
•Pay your personal bills

Note: Capital one 360 Accounts allow you to do this

The amounts that you decide upon will accumulate over time. As a result, there is money in the tax account to pay quarterlies and stay on top of taxes.

Checking and Savings		Balance
360 Checking - Personal		$2,875.21
360 Savings - Rainy Day		$2,894.87
360 Saving - Taxes		$7,491.23
360 Savings - Retirement		$5,791.03
360 Savings - Travel and Leisure		$3,191.56
360 Savings - Savings		$31,257.69

As you build your business, look to add additional revenue streams. This creates diversity and helps you build passive income.

Real Estate Sales

Team

Your Business

Profit Share

Investments
Properties
Stocks
Business
Market Center

Balance

Many agents are reactionary. We spend our days reacting to issues, leads and so on. We answer the phone in the evenings and on the weekends. We fear losing the sale or the lead.

Many times we have no idea where we are in our business. What our required sales production is, number of sides needed, average commission, how much further we have to go. This creates anxiety and stress which will suck the energy out of you and will have a negative impact.

If you are dealing with personal issues, most of the time, it affects your business; if you are dealing with business issues, it affects your personal life. You must separate the two, remove the emotional ties to the business. Still have feelings but do not allow the stress to overtake you. Never forget that you are a professional and paid to handle your emotions. Make time for your family, friends, hobbies etc. Otherwise the business will consume you and you will become obsessed. Nothing will matter except the business, which will have a negative impact on relationships and your personal life.

(In the final series, we will tie it all together with goals, planning and tracking which will create balance.)

In order to reduce stress, identify 3 things that, if eliminated,
would make your life better.

1._____

2._____

3._____

© Copyright 2016 MoreGCI.com All rights reserved
No part of this ebook may be reproduced, distributed, or transmitted in any form or by any means, including photocopying, recording, or other electronic or mechanical methods, without the prior written permission of MoreGCI, except in the case of brief quotations embodied in critical reviews and certain other noncommercial uses permitted by copyright law.

Control Your Time

In your business sector, you need to teach your clients your availability.

Be available until 6pm via phone, email and text unless it is a negotiating circumstance, otherwise they will not respect your time.

Pick which days/evenings work best to schedule appointments and stick to it as much as possible. I try to schedule appointments on Tuesday, Thursday and Saturday mornings or Monday and Wednesday afternoons.

I take 1-2 half days during the week; it gives me something to look forward to.

In your personal sector, you need to shut the business off. If you need a second person, get one. If you have your own team, you may want a team phone and each weekend, someone else takes the phone. It is only for business and by doing so, it reduces the stress to any one person.

When you are fresh from enjoying life you will be better for your clients. When you are balanced in your business sector and making money, personal life is so much better.

We start business to create Freedom, not to create Bondage for ourselves.

The More GCI Agent Manager

The More GCI Agent Manager will also help with balance. It organizes your numbers so you can understand, track and convert your leads as well as track follow up and so much more.

This allows you to take your mind off everything else and focus on things of importance: your purpose, your passion, your family, your business and YOU.

Goals & Action Plans

Goals are the most important things you must complete in order to achieve success. Without goals, you will not have a clear idea of what you are trying to achieve.

Your goals need to be well thought out, attainable and in writing. Otherwise they are dreams. While dreams are nice to have, it's better to have a dream come true than a dream in your head.

You need to create goals for:

- # Business — Our Focus with More GCI.
- # Personal
- # Financial
- # Family
- # Spiritual / Religious

You must also be able to track those goals to know whether you are on track to reach them and adjust when needed. No one knows or understands how hard you work to achieve these goals or how much work goes into being successful except you.

If you set and track goals, you now need to be held accountable. Accountability + Discipline = Success.

Start Making Goals NOW!

Net Income	100,000	
Tax Rate	20.00%	
Income B4 Taxes		125,000
Cap	27,500	
Royalty	3,000	
Business Expenses	12,000	
Adjusted Gross		167,500
Avg Com %	2.50%	
Avg Sales Price	400,000	
Production Required		6,700,000
Number of sides Yr	16.75	
Mo	1.40	

How much do you need to make?

*Personal $_____

*Business $_____

Total $_____

* From your earlier budget

It has been said that goals have different levels and many micro-goals to achieve. For instance, if you want to make **$100,000 a year** and your average sales commission is **$5,000,** you will need **20** sales per year.

Which is **1.6 per month**, so the micro goal, as a result, is **1.6 sales per month**.

So your Micro goal is **3-4 appointments per month**, that's less than **1 per week**.

Your main focus **each Monday** should be to set an appointment with a **new Buyer or new Seller**.

That's it…

If you achieve this, you will achieve the greater goal!

Goal

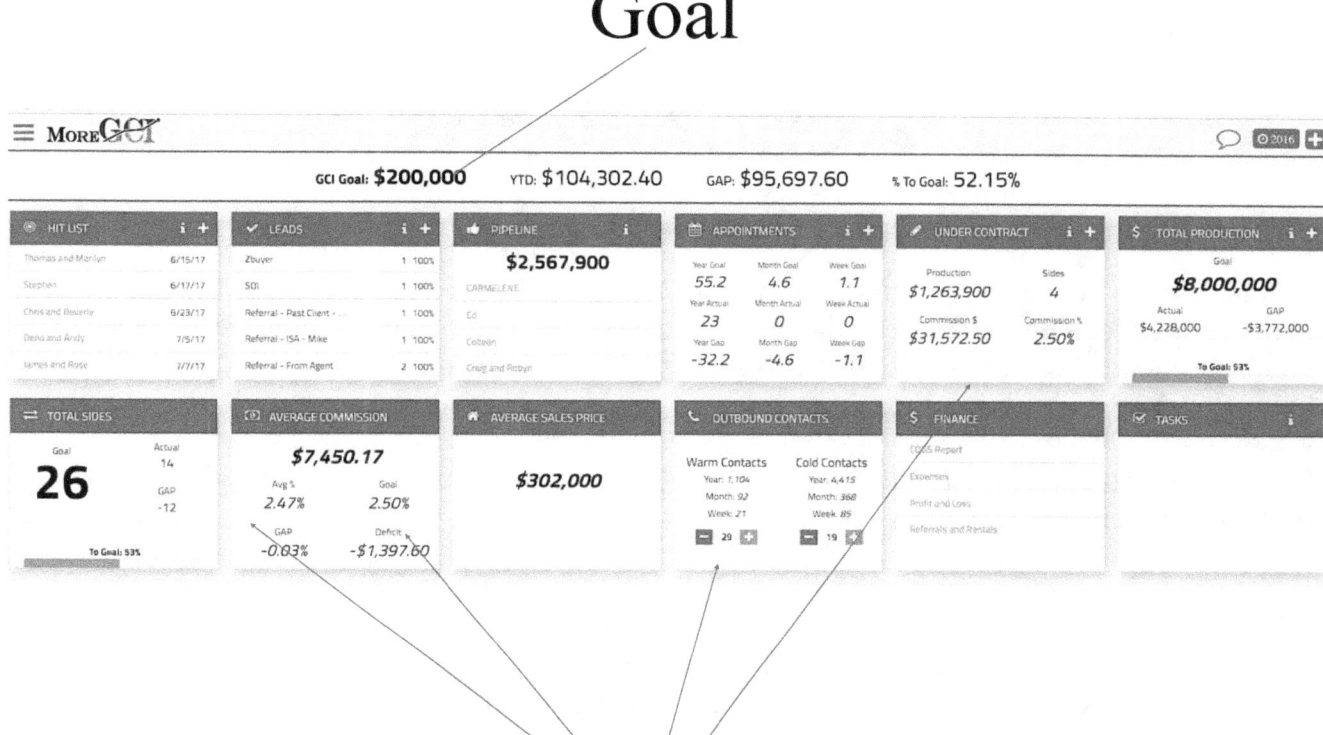

Micro Goals

- **Smart** – Gives me the quality of life I desire
- **Measurable** – It is tracked throughout the year
- **Realistic** – Definitely attainable
- **Specific** – Income goal is then broken into smaller goals
- **Time Bound** – Per year
- **Agreed** – The amount that is determined to give me the results I want

Action Plans

If goals are the desired destinations, an Action Plan is the GPS to get you there. To create goals with no idea how to achieve them is not following the principals of goal setting. Once you have Smart, Measurable, Realistic, Specific, Time Bound and Agreed goals, you need to know how you will achieve them.

So you have plugged in your Goals (the destination) and the Action Plan (GPS) gives you a route to get there.

An action plan will show you:

- Who to call and follow up with
- How much business you are working on
- How many contacts you need
- How many appointments you need

While there is some overlap of Micro Goals and Action Plans, there are differences.

Take Appointments; The micro goal is 3-4 appointments per month, as in the above example. So the Action Plan is to call, email, text, network or whatever you need to do to get that appointment. If you need 33 Warm contacts or 100 Cold contacts per week, you make those contacts until you achieve the result… An appointment.

Action Plan

Action Plan

Action Plans also allow you to see what is required in order to achieve the goal.

•**Hit List** is for your follow ups… The $$ is in the follow up.
•**Pipeline** is the tangible business at your finger tips.
•**Appointments** are the number of appointments you need.
•**Outbound Contacts** are the number of contacts you need to achieve each week, broken down to warm and cold.

MORE
GCI

Accountability

Goals and Action Plans ONLY work if you are held accountable. You need to have an accountability partner or a system like More GCI to track those goals and be held accountable. Failure to be held accountable will sway you from the path of success.

Agents who hold themselves accountable, or who are held accountable by another, achieve better success than agents who do not. Accountability coupled with Discipline to DO WHAT IS REQUIRED will lead to SUCCESS. Without Accountability and Discipline you will find Frustration.

In a business structure, it is the manager who would holds you Accountable. The More GCI Agent Manager will be able to hold you Accountable for organizing your business, goals and action plans. You must implement Discipline in order to achieve success. Discipline is also the 4th principal we discussed in part 1, the UPAD Principals of Success

We have broken your success down to the simple… the easy…. All you need to do is have Discipline to log and do what it tells you, once a day or at least 2-3 times a week. Follow the road map and succeed.

What tools or systems do you have in place to stay accountable?

_____

Who holds you accountable? Do you have an accountability partner or coach?

_____

Lead Generation & Follow Up

Some would argue that lead generation is the most important activity we can accomplish all day. I agree to a point but want to dig deeper. Follow Up is the most important thing we can do daily.

You get a lead.. You call, maybe even meet and do a listing presentation. Only to see the property listed 2 months later with another agent. Then it dawns on you… I have not called them since our meeting… After all, they said they would call ME… The nerve…

If there is any one thing I want you to walk away with:

The money is in the FOLLOW UP!

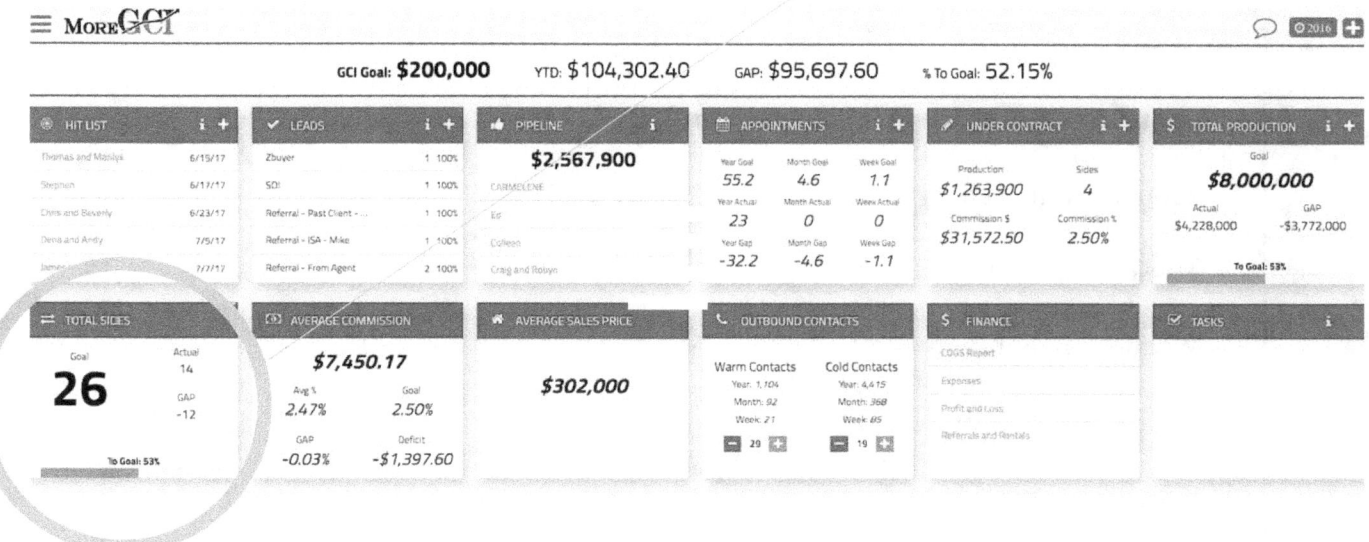

Follow Up

Increase your chances by having better follow up. Know when to call and who to call and never forget to call again.

I am sure you have written names on napkins, bags, scrap paper, body parts or whatever was available. You need to immediately put them into your system and increase your chances. You worked hard for that lead… In many cases, there is a cost to procure that lead. Help yourself.

To start, schedule 2-3 one hour blocks per week and follow up. Only make follow up calls during this time.

Do you currently time block?

Yes / No

What Days / Times work best for you? Pick 3 now:

- Monday am / pm

- Tuesday am / pm

- Wednesday am / pm

- Thursday am / pm

- Friday am / pm

MORE GCI

With Goals, Action Plans, Accountability, Discipline and the right system, Success is possible.

Starting Point

≡ MORE GCI   ○ 2016 ＋

| GCI Goal: **$200,000** | YTD: $104,302.40 | GAP: $95,697.60 | % To Goal: 52.15% |

HIT LIST i +

Thomas and Marilyn	6/15/17
Stephen	br'7/17
Chris and Beverly	6/23/17
Dona and Andy	/17
James and Rose	7/7/17

LEADS i +

Zbuyer	1	100%
SOI	1	100%
Referral - Past Client - . .	1	100%
Referral - ISA - Mike	1	100%
Referral - From Agent	2	100%

PIPELINE i

$2,567,900

CARMELENE
Ed
Colleen
Craig and Robyn

APPOINTMENTS i +

Year Goal	Month Goal	Week Goal
55.2	4.6	1.1
Year Actual	Month Actual	Week Actual
23	0	0
Year Gap	Month Gap	Week Gap
-32.2	-4.6	-1.1

UNDER CONTRACT i +

Production	Sides
$1,263,900	4
Commission $	Commission %
$31,572.50	2.50%

TOTAL PRODUCTION $ i +

Goal
$8,000,000

Actual	GAP
$4,228,000	-$3,772,000

To Goal: 53%

TOTAL SIDES

Goal	Actual
26	14
	GAP
	-12

To Goal: 53%

AVERAGE COMMISSION

$7,450.17

Avg %	Goal
2.47%	2.50%
GAP	Deficit
-0.03%	-$1,397.60

AVERAGE SALES PRICE

$302,000

OUTBOUND CONTACTS

Warm Contacts	Cold Contacts
Year: 1,104	Year: 4,415
Month: 92	Month: 368
Week: 21	Week: 85
− 29 ＋	− 19 ＋

FINANCE $

COGS Report
Expenses
Profit and Loss
Referrals and Rentals

TASKS i

SUCCESS =
1. Receive and convert leads
2. Put under contract
3. Close
4. Repeat

Goals and Action Plans coupled with Accountability and Discipline are the only thing that will bring you to where you want to be.

They will create a road map (Action Plan) showing what you need to do to be successful. Accountability and Discipline will keep you on the right path...

Plan your goals and create an action plan…

Follow it…

Track it…

Achieve it…

Note: The leap of faith is exciting, scary, frustrating, rewarding and many other feelings (adjectives?). Successful people say I can do it. Fear holds most of us back but those. In Science, for every negative there is a positive. Those who use Fear as a positive motivational force, achieve success. Those who use fear as a crutch, fail.

Write down Goals you want to accomplish this year in both Business and Personal. What do you need to do in order to achieve them? What are your challenges and action plans? Log what you've accomplished or why you weren't able to accomplish them and your adjustment plan.

Business Goal

Sales and Production Goals   GCI _____ Sides_____ (if a team use team goals)

Needs / Challenges_____

Action Plan_____

Accomplished Y/N If Yes Date _____If No Why?_____

Adjustment Plan_____

Business Growth

New team members in production _____ Admin_____ ISA_____ TC_____

Needs / Challenges_____

Action Plan_____

Accomplished Y/N If Yes Date _____If No Why?_____

Adjustment Plan_____

Passive Income Growth

Members added to Downline_____

Needs / Challenges_____

Action Plan_____

Accomplished Y/N If Yes Date _____If No Why?_____

Adjustment Plan_____

Personal Goals

1. _____Accomplish By:_____

Needs / Challenges_____

Action Plan_____

Accomplished Y/N If Yes Date _____If No Why?_____

Adjustment Plan_____

2. _____ Accomplish By:_____

Needs / Challenges_____

Action Plan_____

Accomplished Y/N If Yes Date _____If No Why?_____

Adjustment Plan_____

3. _____ Accomplish By:_____

Needs / Challenges_____

Action Plan_____

Accomplished Y/N If Yes Date _____If No Why?_____

Adjustment Plan_____

Ideas: Vacation, Savings, New Vehicle, Camper, Investment Property, Invest in other MC's, College Tuition...

Put some thought into this. Write them down, write the challenge down. Find the solution and achieve it.

Put this page where you can see it every day. As you accomplish the goals, check them off. At the end of the year review and see your accomplishments or adjust the action plan as needed.

Blank for Note Taking

www.ingramcontent.com/pod-product-compliance
Lightning Source LLC
Chambersburg PA
CBHW081228170526
45165CB00009B/2999